Places
in My Neighborhood

by Shelly Lyons

Consulting Editor: Gail Saunders-Smith, PhD

CAPSTONE PRESS
a capstone imprint

Pebble Books are published by Capstone Press,
1710 Roe Crest Drive, North Mankato, Minnesota 56003
www.capstonepub.com

Library of Congress Cataloging-in-Publication Data
Lyons, Shelly.
 Places in my neighborhood / by Shelly Lyons.
p. cm. — (Pebble plus. My neighborhood)
ISBN 978-1-62065-100-1 (library binding)
ISBN 978-1-62065-885-7 (paperback)
ISBN 978-1-4765-1723-0 (eBook PDF)
 1. Neighborhoods—Juvenile literature. 2. Communities—Juvenile literature. I. Title.
HM756.L96 2013
 307.3'362—dc23   2012023418

Editorial Credits
Sarah Bennett, designer; Svetlana Zhurkin, media researcher; Danielle Ceminsky, production specialist

Photo Credits
Capstone Studio: Karon Dubke, 11, 13, 15, 19, 21; Dreamstime: Tom Fawls, cover; iStockphotos: DNY59, 9,
Jay Lazarin, 5, phi2, 17; Shutterstock: A-R-T (background), 1 and throughout, trekandshoot, 7

Note to Parents and Teachers

The My Neighborhood set supports social studies standards related to community. This
book describes and illustrates places in a neighborhood. The images support early readers in
understanding the text. The repetition of words and phrases helps early readers learn new words.
This book also introduces early readers to subject-specific vocabulary words, which are defined in
the Glossary section. Early readers may need assistance to read some words and to use the Table of
Contents, Glossary, Read More, Internet Sites, and Index sections of the book.

Table of Contents

What Is a Neighborhood? . . . 4

Places to Live 6

Places to Keep Us Safe 10

Places to Find Things 16

Glossary 22

Read More 23

Internet Sites 23

Index .24

What Is a Neighborhood?

A neighborhood is a
community filled with
different places to see.
Each place has a special
purpose that meets our needs.

Places to Live

Mia's home is in the city.

Her apartment is in a building with many other apartments.

Jack lives in a house

in a small town.

His street is lined with homes.

Places to Keep Us Safe

Carlos visits the fire station

in his neighborhood.

The firefighters rush

to put out a fire.

Devon visits the police station.

The officer tells him

not to talk to strangers.

POLICE STATION

POLICE
PUBLIC SAFETY

13

At the clinic,

a nurse gives Lila a shot.

She feels better when

she gets a bandage.

Places to Find Things

Justin bikes to the library

in his neighborhood.

He checks out books

about dinosaurs.

Jen wants fruit and milk.

At the grocery store

her dad finds fresh grapefruit.

19

Neighborhoods can be big or small. What places do you see in your neighborhood?

Glossary

apartment—a home that has its own rooms and front door, but which shares outside walls and a roof with other apartments

bandage—a covering that protects cuts and wounds

community—a group of people who live in the same area

grocery store—a store that sells food items

station—a place or building where a certain service is based

Read More

Mayer, Cassie. *Homes*. Our Global Community. Chicago: Heinemann Library, 2007.

Owens, L. L. *Meet Your Neighborhood*. Let's Be Social. Edina, Minn.: Magic Wagon, 2011.

Schuh, Mari C. *In My Neighborhood*. My World. Mankato, Minn.: Capstone Press, 2006.

Internet Sites

FactHound offers a safe, fun way to find Internet sites related to this book. All of the sites on FactHound have been researched by our staff.

Here's all you do:

Visit *www.facthound.com*

Type in this code: 9781620651001

Super-cool stuff!

Check out projects, games and lots more at
www.capstonekids.com

Index

apartments, 6

clinics, 14

communities, 4

firefighters, 10

fire stations, 10

grocery stores, 18

homes, 6, 8

houses, 8

libraries, 16

nurses, 14

police officers, 12

police stations, 12

Word Count: 140
Grade: 1
Early-Intervention Level: 16